12

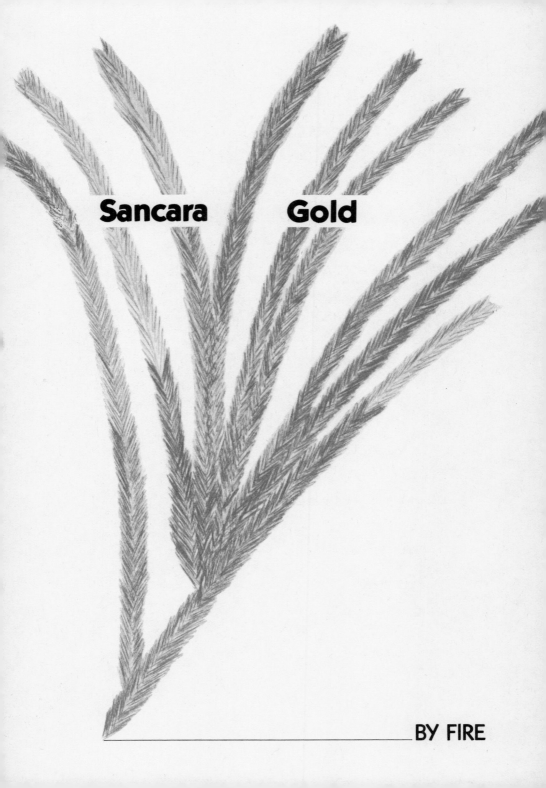

Sancara Gold

BY FIRE

FIRST EDITION

SHŬ PUBLISHING
P.O. BOX 779
WEST SIDE STATION
WORCESTER, MASSACHUSETTS, 01602
        USA

ISBN   0-938885-49-9

Library of Congress Cataloging-in-Publication Data

Fire, 1943-
    Sancara gold.

    I. Title.
PS3556.I6S26 1990   811'.54   90-9081
ISBN 0-938885-49-9

THIS BOOK IS DEDICATED TO
ALL WHO LIVE ETERNITY IN THE MOMENT
WITH THE COURAGE TO TOUCH PROFOUNDLY
THE SOUL OF ANOTHER .

BLACK WOLF WOMYN
COME DOWN INTO THIS ORANGE
CAULDRON
& FIND WHERE THE MOON HIDES
HER SILVER POWER

A GOLDEN GIRL FLIES
THRU THE WINDS
OF MY MIND

1   WE MEET ON THE EDGE
2   BLACK SANDS $$$ SOFT LIPS
3   SACRED BEAUTY $$$ SACRED WOMYN
4   MALACCA TEMPLE
5   DJANET MASSIF
6   BIRD WOMYN
7   BLUE DRAGON
8   GOLD RIDERS
9   BEYOND EARTHWALK
10 WIND WHISPERS
              $$$$$$$$$$
11 GOLD RIVERS
12 SILVER WIND
13 SACRED SILENCES
14 WHIRLING DERVISHES
15 FIRE DRUMS
16 RED FOXES
17 LAVA FIRE $$$ GARLIC/LEMON $$$
              BLUE FIRE
18 SILVER RED $$$ GOLDEN MOONLIGHT
19 INTERIOR JUNGLE GORGES $$$
                 MIDNIGHT SUN
20 LION DANCER
          $$$$$$$$$$
21 ORANGE WOLF MOON
22 HER ELEGANT SEASONS OF MIST
23 SILVER & GOLD WOMYN
24 LIQUID LOVERS
25 BRANDY SNIFTERS OF RUBY GARNET
26 BLACK DIAMONDS $$$ FLOWING GOLD
27 BANDS ACROSS THE MOON
28 MALACHITE / BASKET OF BLOODSTONES
29 BLUE WOMYN (WIND WALKER)
30 BLUE WOLF

31 BLUE EYES
32 CORAL SNAKE
33 TIBETAN TURQUOISE
34 LOVE LIVES IN THE SILENCES
35 ORANGE SNAKES
36 AZTEC GODDESS
37 AMBER MOMENTS
38 PURPLE/GOLD WHISPERS
39 TSURIGANE
40 MAGENTA GOLD
    $$$$$$$$$
41 WILD INDIGO LOVER
42 SPRING SNOW
43 MAGENTA VOICE
44 BLACK LAKES & SERPENT RIVERS
45 BLUE SKIN
46 WOLF WALKING THE DARKNESS
47 WOLF WALKING THE DARKNESS P.2
48 MOCCASIN WOMYN
49 RAINBOW CITIES
50 KASHMIR SUNSETS
    $$$$$$$$$
51 PURPLE GARDENS
52 LAKOTA BUDDHIST MESSAGES
53 CRYSTAL RAIN
54 SUMMER RAIN
55 ELLEGGUA-ELEGBA
56 LEMON CAVES
57 PINK DAWN
58 WEST WIND OUT OF SUMATRA
59 DREAMING INTO HER OPENINGS
60 LAVENDAR FREEDOMS

61 DIAMOND MYSTERIES $$ VELVET WOMYN
62 DATE PALM
63 DRINKING GOURD
64 HARLEQUIN WOMYN
65 VEILED SURFACES
66 PURPLE PATHWAYS
67 GOLD & COPPER GIRAFFES
68 YOU ARE MAKING ME CRAZY
69 HONEY LEMON
70 BIRDS OF PARADISE
         $$$$$$$$$
71 LA GANA
72 XONCHITO
73 AGIYA
74 BOUNCING BUBBLES
75 MOONLIGHT RAIN
76 HURRICANE WAVES
77 SILENT MYSTERY $$$ FREE ME
78 BLACK AS THE NIGHT
80 SPRING FLAMES
         $$$$$$$$$
81 OUT OF THE WHIRLWIND
82 REGGAE MEMORIES
83 VOID OF THE DREAMERS
84 MIRROR MASK
85 GOLD & SILVER TRIANGLES
86 UNKNOWN MYSTERIES $$$ OTHER WORLDS
87 BLUE GREY RIDGES
88 SACRED WARRIOR SONG
89 TOMORROW
90 HER EXISTENCE $$ ILLUSION OF A MOMENT
91 WALKING BEYOND
92 BORDERS
93 LIGHTENING $$$ FIRE WALKER

WE MEET ON THE EDGE
OF DARKNESS
WHERE TIME & SPACE
HAVE NO MEASURE

YOUR LAVENDAR BODY
WALKS WAVES
OF MORNING

& YOUR LIQUID MOTION
HAS CREATED
THE RISING SUN

OUR LOVE IS
BLACK SANDS
OF
JAGGED SOFTNESS

SOFT LIPS
ACROSS DESERT
MOUNTAIN RIDGES
SHE STANDS
ON SAND DUNES
SURROUNDED
BY WOLF POWER

2

SHE IS EXQUISITE
SACRED BEAUTY

SHE IS SACRED
EXOTIC WOMYN

WITH VOICE TONES
THAT AMPLIFY
THE SUN

MY DREAM WOMYNS SPICES
PERFUME MALAYSIAN CLOUDS
IN GREEN TEMPLES
OF MALACCA

HER ESSENCE IS OBSERVATION &
                    INTROSPECTION

THIS UNIQUE/INSPIRING WOMYN
OF EXQUISITE FASCINATION

A NEVER-ENDING DREAM
LOST IN PINK SALT
BENEATH
A DJANET
MASSIF

BIRD WOMYN
YOU HAVE PUT WINGS
TO THE STILLNESS
OF INTROSPECTION

A BLUE DRAGON LIVES IN
MY GOLD RIVER

IT RAGES
BLOOD RED
FIRE

FROM THE RIDERS ON
THE DARK SIDE OF
THE MOON

       GOLD   GOLD
       RED   GOLD

WITH LIGHTENING BOLTS
EMANATING FROM
THE SIDES OF
THEIR SKULLS

       GOLD   GOLD
       GOLD RAYS

ITS PURPLE ON
THE DARK SIDE OF THE MOON
& THEY RIDE SILVER HORSES

MY WOMYN TRAVELS WILD / & FREE
FOLLOWING A PATH
TO DESTINATIONS
BEYOND THIS EARTHWALK

I FEEL HER
WHISPERS
IN THE WIND

GOLD RIVERS SPIRAL
RELEASING YOUR
BLACK DIAMONDS

/

WOMYN

I LIVE YOU IN FIRE
ORANGE/RED HEAT
BLACK ICE
SILVER WIND ABOVE
THE TIMBER LINE

DARLING
THAT PASSION
RAGES IN YOU
JUST BELOW
YOUR SURFACES
IT LAYERS
VOLCANO
COLORS /   HEAT /
POWER

YOUR SCENT IS MORE
APHRODISIAC
THAN A TRILLION FLOWERS
GROWING MADLY
ACROSS THE RIDGES
OF DISTANT GALAXIES

GOLDEN WORLDS HAVE ALWAYS EXISTED
BUT HAVE WE
REMEMBERED THE RED BORDERS
OF OUR MINDS
THAT CREATE GEOMETRIC PATTERNS
OF INDUCTIONS /
PRAYERS IN SOUND PATTERNS
LEAP THE BOUNDARIES CREATED
BY COLORS OF THE MORNING /
SAILS OF SACRED SILENCES
CONTROL YOUR BORDERS
& SPACE EXPANDS FOREVER IN YOUR
VISION /

I HAVE WALKED CRYSTAL WORLDS
OF OTHER GALAXIES
I HAVE SEEN THE WINDS
OF WHIRLING DERVISHES
COMPETE FOR THE POWER
OF YOUR MIND

THUNDER WOMYN

   WITH
   LIGHTENING & MOONLIGHT
    IN HER EYES

TRAVELS EAGLE PATHS

DANCES FIRE DRUMS

MOVES THRU LIQUID
  LIKE WIND

SHE IS LIKE BEING IMMERSED
        IN SWEETGRASS

A VAST PRAIRIE
     FIRED
     TO A PURIFYING INCENSE

MOVING RED FOXES
ONTO PERIMETERS

16

HER LAVA FIRE
IGNITES
A JADE SKY

GARLIC/LEMON
RED PEPPER WOMYN
ON YOUR SACRED ALTAR
I BURN
PURPLE & GOLD
CANDLE / FLAMES

THE BLUE FIRE
EXISTS IN LEMON CAVES
LOST BENEATH THE SEA

17

SHE PAINTS SUMMER
MOON
SILVER RED

THE WIND HAS BECOME
FLOWING SILK
& SHE IS GOLDEN
MOONLIGHT

18

HER BEAUTIFUL INTERIOR JUNGLE GORGES
CREATE SPEEDING UNIVERSAL JOURNEYS

I HAVE BECOME
LIKE THE SUN
AT MIDNIGHT

LION DANCER

SWEET APRIL LOVER   /
MOVE ASIDE THE VEILS
& LET THE RAINS COME

BRING THE MAGNIFICENT
COLORS OF FOREVERS

WRAP THE WORLD IN GOLD

REMEMBER YOUR DREAM
& A TURQUOISE PATH
WILL FLOW BENEATH
THE ORANGE WOLF MOON

LIVE YOUR VISIONS

IN BEAUTY
    POWER
    & LOVE

TOTALLY ENRAPTURED
IN ADMIRING PERFECT SILENCE
I CONTEMPLATE HER NATURAL
GRACEFUL BEAUTY

ABSORBED BY REVELATION
I AM HUMBLED BY DISCOVERY
OF **HER ELEGANT**
SEASONS OF MIST

SILVER & GOLD WOMYN
CARRY THE DREAM

LIVE IN SMOKY CLOUDS
IN FRONT OF THE MOON

FLOAT RAINBOW SKIES
OF BLUE CRYSTALS

LIQUID LOVERS
START THEIR DAY
FLOATING WAVES
ACROSS WATER-BEDS
MASSAGING LIQUID ABDOMENS
FROM PAPEETE/TAHITI TO
CARIBBEAN MADNESS
ON YOUR FRECKLED BROWN SKIN

TROPICAL FOUNTAINS SPRAY MAGENTA/
                    GREEN STARS

AS YOU LIE ON THE DESERT
WOMYN
WITH YOUR HARDENING SECRETS
OF MORNING MADNESS
& WE RIDE THE WAVES
INTO OTHER WORLDS
OF CHAINED
LEATHER
BITING WOLVES
                    /

24

GOLDEN WOMYN
I DRINK YOUR SWEETNESS
IN BRANDY SNIFTERS
OF RUBY GARNET

BLUE CRYSTAL WATERFALLS
EMBELLISH MY SOUL

& MOTION IS AS PERPETUAL
AS A DESERT ROCK LIZARD
WAITING FOR THE SUN

GOLDEN RIVERS
SPIRAL
RELEASING
BLACK DIAMONDS

SHE IS SWEET

FLOWING GOLD

I WANT TO PAINT BANDS ACROSS THE MOON
MY LOVER

I WANT TO GATHER STAR DIAMONDS
IN THEIR SOFT BRILLIANT GLOW

& LIVE A FREE POWER
THAT IS SACRED

IS EVERYWHERE
IS COMPLETE

OH MY WOMYN
THE WAY YOU LOVE
IS SO POWERFUL   /
THE MYSTERY OF OUR LOVE IS
A MALACHITE CENTER
IN A BASKET OF BLOODSTONES

I
  O WIND WALKER
FROM THE LAND OF THE WESTERN DREAM
COME
TO ME
UNDER THESE BRANCHES
& LISTEN
TO THE MAGIC
BEAUTY OF THE RAIN
IT BATHES US IN
DIAMOND SPARKLED LIQUID

II
  JOY/TOMATOES/ DAHL/KUM-KUM   /
PEPPERS /PERSIMMONS /PASSION

BLUE/ORANGE KOHL OUTLINED SKY

III
  BLUE WOMYN /   WE ARE ONE

                ////

                  ///

                    //

BLUE WOLF RAGING
    DOWN THE RIDGES
        OF PAIN

YOU LUNGE
    YOUR PROTECTION

WHEN   UNIVERSAL LAWS
    HAVE BEEN BROKEN

WOLVES WALK IN SILVER MOONLIGHT
WITH THEIR BLUE EYES FLASHING

SHE IS CORAL SNAKE
USING HER SHED SKINS
AS THE DIAMOND BACKED RATTLER
WARNING YOU
WITH HER SOUNDS
        HER COLORS

GIVING YOU
A CHANCE
TO GET AWAY

MY SPINE IS FROZEN
INLAID TIBETAN TURQUOISE
THAT SHE CARESSES TO LIFE

LOVE LIVES IN THE SILENCES
COMMUNICATES WITH THE EYES
IN THE SOUND TONES
FROM ANOTHER TIME

RED GOLD TRIANGLES
SEND YELLOW LIGHT
TO MY HEART /

GREEN EYES DEFINE MYSTERIES /

/

ORANGE SNAKES SING ME HOME
TO STARS
ON MARKED MIDNIGHT LAKES

RED/ YELLOW/ ORANGE/ SUN WOMYN
GOLDEN EAGLE SPIRIT
CALLS AZTEC GODDESS
FROM BLUE BODIES OF POWER

BIRD WOMYN PAINTING GOLD
BEYOND CLOUDS /

36

SHE IS A BROWN SKIN WOMYN
WITH A VOICE LIKE MIDNIGHT
& SPARKLING DIAMOND GREEN EYES
OF UNDISCOVERED PLANETS

WALK THOSE WOLF PATHS DARLING

WEAR YOUR AMBER MOMENTS
WITH THE BEAUTY OF   MYSTERIOUS
                        JEWELS

WE LIVE BENEATH THE WATERS OF
        WILD RIVERS

ENCODED WITH MESSAGES OF ANCIENT
                GALAXIES
YET TO BE
        DISCOVERED
                /

EBONY INLAID
LOTUS WOMYN

PURPLE / GOLD WHISPERS
RIDE ON SUMMER WINDS

38

*TSURIGANE

_____

ENIGMATIC
TEXTS OF GOLD
VIOLET ROBED
HAUNTING IRIS FLUTE MELODIES   /
INCENSE SPICED
MY RED LION WOMYN
YOUR BRONZE ALTAR OF
LACQUERED DRAGONS &
LOTUS CHERRY BLOSSOMS
CONCEAL
FOXES
   LOST IN
      PLUM /   BAMBOO
            BEYONDS
                  /

  *THE GREAT TEMPLE BELL OF NOGIYAMA

MAGENTA GOLD

SHE SPEAKS TIME IN MANY LANGUAGES
& ALL OF THEM HAVE ORIGINATED BEHIND
THE SUN /   PERFECTED AMONG THE MOONS
OF CONSTANT RENAISSANCE
ALL-ENCLOSING WOMYN
REACHING THE FOYER OF
MY MIND
WHERE COLORES WAIT TO BE
PAINTED   /   BLENDED INTO BLUE RHYTHMS
THAT HAVE LOOKED BEYOND LIMITS
& FLED THE MOMENTS MADNESS /
HEAR THE TRAIN BLOW LONESOME
WHISTLE STOPS   &
FLY ON ROLLER COASTER
FLOWER PRINTS INTO
MID-NIGHT SILVER LAKES
A GOLD WOMYN FLASHES
IN BLINDING MOVEMENTS
THAT CIRCLE EARTH-EYES
CREATING A CAPELLA REASONS
TO SEEK THE SUN
LOST IN MAGENTA RAYS
& THOSE BLUE/VIOLET SPIRALS KEEP MOVING
INTO TOMORROWS
& TURQUOISE DREAMS
BLEND EVERYTHING
INTO ONE ESSENCE   /
ONLY ONE EFFORT CAN SUSTAIN
& ILLUMINATE THE MOMENTS
OF PROGRESSION   /
WHEN WERE THE BARRIERS CROSSED
& WHERE WERE THE GUIDEPOSTS
ENCOUNTERED   /
AWAKENED TO BEAUTY
MY SOUL REVELED IN ECSTASY
& SANG TO GENTLENESS   /

40

SHE IS MY WILD INDIGO LOVER
YELLOW SUNLIGHT
PURPLE PASSION
IMITATING
UNTIL MY TRUE LOVE RETURNS
TO COLOR MY LIFE
FLAME RED

PART I

         SPRING SNOW IS SO MAGICAL
         LIKE YOU SO MAGICAL
         LIKE A WOLF IN THE SNOW
         A DEER IN THE FOREST
         YOU ARE THE WILDNESS OF NATURE
         THE BEAUTY OF NATURE
         AS COMPLEX AS MYRIADS OF
                      SNOW CRYSTALS
         AS ICE HOT AS SNOW BANKING
         THE IGLOO WOMB OF MY MIND

PART II

         DARLING HOW CAN I UNDERSTAND
                           ART
         WHEN YOU ARE SO REAL
         UNDERSTATED
         ONGOING
         EXQUISITE BEAUTY
         OF RAGING THUNDER
         & GENTLE RABBIT SOFTNESS
         DEFYING DESCRIPTION
         WOMYN
         KNOWN ONLY THRU ENERGY
         FLOWS
         & VAST SILENCES OF MAGNITUDE

PART III

         I GIVE YOU ORANGE & YELLOW
                    FEATHERS
         FOR YOUR SHIELD
         & SWEETGRASS FOR YOUR LIFE /

HER CRYSTAL DIAMOND VOICE
IS A HUGE MAGENTA FLOWER
CASCADING WATERFALLS
BENEATH SILVERMOON

BLACK LAKES & SERPENT RIVERS
LIVE IN MY BLOOD
SUN RIDGES PAINT
DUSK ACROSS THE PATTERNS OF MY SOUL

& YOU / YOU SHUN DZU
WHERE HAVE YOU FLED
IN DRAGON BOATS
ACROSS TEMPLE COVERED BRIDGES
TO THE SWEET LOTUS
OF MEMORY
TIGER STEMS HAVE ENSNARED
MY SOUL'S DELIGHT
& THE MOON HAS GREETED STARS
BEYOND RAINBOWS

YOU ARE THE MYSTERY /

BLACK SILVER FLASHES
& A GOLD WORLD APPEARS
BEHIND THE MAGENTA PUPILS
OF YOUR EYES /

WOMYN/ YOUR BLUE SKIN
CREATES AN ICE PURPLE AURA /

THE SHADOW OF YOUR DARKNESS

                                    /
                                      /
                                        /

45

THIS WOLF WALKING THE DARKNESS
OF THE DREAMTIME
WAVES CIRCLE SLOWLY INTO
THE VASTNESS OF CONCENTRIC MINDS /
& YOUR EYES
RECEIVING THE POWER
OF OTHER WORLDS /   MOVE INTO
THE OPENINGS
HOWLING DOWN
RAGING DOWN
THE HIMALAYAS
& LEOPARDS OF SNOW
CENTER INTO TIBETAN GRAVES
OF ORANGE DOORWAYS /
WHERE ARE THE WHEELS THAT SPIN THE GREEN
COLORS   INTO AN ETERNITY & BEYOND
/ O WALKER OF THE SNOW-BOUND NIGHT
SKYWAYS DETAIN YOU
AS YOU APPROACH THE TEMPLE
DOORWAYS INLAID WITH EBONY
MASKS UNCOVERED AT
THE MOMENT OF CONCEPTION
CRIES OF WONDERMENT HAVE STALKED
THESE RIDGES OF ANGLED AVALANCHES
IN SECRETS
UNDER-TOWED TO THE BLUE
LIQUID TOUCHING
PINK BAYS /
O WOMYN
WHY ARE THE CRYSTALS HIDDEN /
UNTIL THE POWER HAS SURFACED &
AGED INTO ROCKWAYS
THAT KNOW NO EDGES
/ O GIRL WALKING RIVERS
THAT HAVE PASSED
FOR TIMES LOADED QUESTIONS
& YOU NOW ARE KNOWING
HOW POWER IS FLOWING

INTO A MADNESS BORNE
ONTO SUNSET HIGHWAYS
& PURPLE BEACHES
CONDENSED INTO
TOMORROW RAYS
OF BIRD FLYING
INTO EAGLE PATHWAYS
BEYOND THE SCOPE OF
HUNTERS GUNS /
ENDLESS THOUGH WINDS TREES
HAVE FALLEN INTO
BRIDGES /   YOU CAN CROSS
INTO THE RAINBOW &
FIND THE QUESTIONS
GUARDING LIPS THAT HAVE KNOWN
ONLY PURITY
ONLY SACRED
        PLEASURE
& YOU CAN KNEEL AT
GRAVES THAT FOLLOW
GOLDEN MOMENTS
OF AN UNFORSEEN DREAM

///

SHE IS A MOCCASIN WOMYN
BEADING HER WAY
INTO SACRED ROUNDS

GIVING COLOR TO GREY WOLF

48

I LIVE IN RAINBOW CITIES
OF SOFT WHITE DEERSKIN TEEPEES
TURQUOISE SKIES
WITH MAUVE/VIOLET BLENDING
INTO SMOKEY VEILS
OF MOUNTAINS BEYOND THE SUN

OF NIGHT GALAXIES
WHERE DIAMONDS
INTERSPERSE
WITH RUBY MIRAGES
ACROSS THE HORIZON

& DESERT SAND
MEETS PINE RIDGES
ON WINDS OF SMOKE SIGNALS
IN THE POWER OF THE DRUM

THE BLUE WOMYN
ARE ENTHRONED /
GUARDED BY TURNING SNAKES
& FLYING DRAGONS OF HAMMERED GOLD /
PINK KASHMIR SUNSETS
HASTEN THE MOON RAYS
WHERE SECRETS LIVE
IN NIGHT PASSION
& LACQUERED SUNRISE
EXISTS BEYOND
THE FLOWING BLACK GAUZE
OF SKY VEILS

A HUGE BRILLIANT YELLOW SUN EXISTS
BEHIND HER
EMERALD GREEN EYES
BEYOND TIME

THIS RED GLITTER WOMYN
MYSTERIOUS
IN HER SADNESS   /

& I RETURN
TO PURPLE GARDENS
OF PLUM
   BAMBOO
   & PINE
           /

READING ROCKS / LAKOTA BUDDHIST MESSAGES

DIAMOND WOMBS
HAUNT MY MIND
ALMOND BLESSINGS
OF YONI PRAYERS
& THE MYSTICS
CLAIM POWERS
THAT YOU RECEIVE
IN ECSTATIC MOMENTS
WHEN THE VEILS OF ILLUSION
ARE BURNED AWAY

CRYSTAL RAIN
ENCODES
MY MIND MEMORY
FROZEN BEYOND
THE BORDERS
OF TIME

MAGENTA/YELLOW
VIOLET/GREEN
RAINBOWS
LIVE ON POINT
IN THE VAST COLDNESS
OF YOUR BEING   /

I SITTING IN THE DARK
LISTENING TO SUMMER RAIN
OUTSIDE THE OPEN WINDOW

I BECOME THE RAINDROPS

STRETCHED TO MY LIMIT

COMPACTED AS I LAND

COOL ON GREEN LEAVES

II
THE RAIN SILENCES
URBAN NOISE

RETURNS THE CITY
TO THE SACRED

PURIFIES MY
MOMENTS OF BEING

OH BATHE MY SOUL BABY   /
IN THAT MUSIC
CALLING ME BACK
TO DARK RIVER NIGHTS
                        WHERE
THE SOUNDS OF SILENCE

                    LIVE BROADLY
FROM PLANT ANIMAL SPIRITS
                    SPEAKING
TO MY SOUL   /
OH BABY   /   YOU MAKE LOVE
WITH KEYBOARD & DRUM
WHILE YOUR VOICE PRAISES ELLEGGUA_
& MY BODY DANCES DAMBALLAH ELEGBA‾
                              /

MY FINGERS SLIDE
INTO LEMON CAVES
LOST / BENEATH THE SEA

DARLING / I'M CRAVING YOUR
SWEET
LOVE

BEFORE
THE PINK DAWN
FINDS PURPLE PATHWAYS
OF PLEASURE

MY LOVERS COMING
ON A WEST WIND
OUT OF SUMATRA

RING THE BRASS BELLS
CALL DOWN THE POWERS
            OF GOLD

SPREAD RED/ORANGE ROSE PETALS
ON YELLOW SILK

THERE IS A BLUE WOMYN
WALKING THE HILLS OF YESTERDAY

PASSING THRU VIOLET VEILS /

EXPLODING DIAMOND RAINBOWS /

DREAMING INTO HER OPENINGS
I HAVE HAILED THE RISING SUN

OH SWEET MOMENTS
OF THE MYSTERIOUS FOREVER

MOVING MESSAGES OF THE DAWN

DARLING / I LEAVE THE WORLD
TO DESCEND TO THE FREEDOM
OF YOUR
WOLF CAVES
LINED IN RED/LIQUID GOLD
PAST PURPLE METAPHORS
ON BLUE RIVERS
OF LIQUID PASSION
I ENTER DIMENSIONS
RULED BY ENERGY & COLOR
THE LIGHTENING CONNECTS
TO UNIVERSAL FLOWS
IGNITES ENERGIES
FELT ONLY IN ORANGE FIRE   /
TIME MOVES BEYOND LIMITATIONS
& BOUNDARIES ARE
PERCEIVED DIAMONDS
SET IN RUBY CHAINS
OF JADE PEARLS

LOVE WAS DEFINED
IN DIAMOND MYSTERIES

LONG BEFORE
YOU KNEW
THE NIGHT

THE VELVET WOMYN
MOVES IN
DARKENED TUNNELS

SHE IS MY DATE PALM
FEET IN WATER
HEAD IN FIRE

IN THIS GREEN OASIS

WHERE BLACK & WHITE BEETLES
& POISONOUS VIPERS
SEEK OUR GOLD

SHE IS MY DRINKING GOURD
I FOLLOW HER THRU RAINBOW RIVERS

HARLEQUIN WOMYN
DANCING 'CROSS MY MIND
CHANGING MOMENTS
TURNING INSIDE OUT
UPSIDE DOWN
BACKWARD
   &

                            REVERSED

LIFE INTERSECTS WHERE BLACK
CONNECTS WHITE DIAMONDS
'CROSS RED BORDERS TOWNS

SHE VEILS SURFACES
SLOWLY OBLITERATES
DISTANCES

DARLING   I'M CRAVING YOUR
SWEET
LOVE

BEFORE
THE PINK DAWN
FINDS PURPLE PATHWAYS
OF PLEASURE

SHE WALKS AROUND WITH
BLUE LIQUID BETWEEN HER LEGS

& I SEE GOLD & COPPER
                        SHIMMERING
GIRAFFES /
              UPSIDE DOWN

YOU ARE CARVING ME UP BABY
YOU ARE MAKING ME CRAZY

SHE IS HONEY
SWEETNESS
RUNNING
OVER LEMON WEDGES
OF LIFE

SHE EATS CHERRY CHEESECAKE
WITH HER FINGERS
SLIDING PURPLE EGGPLANT
BEYOND HER LIMITS

SHE FLIES WITH BIRDS OF PARADISE
INTO RED/WHITE LILIES

SHE'S LOST IN TIME

70

*   LA GANA

     LA GANA

     OH MY WOMYN

     WHY DO YOU STAY ON THE SURFACE ?

* A STRANGE & INCOMPROMISING DESIRE   /
   CASTILLIAN

*   XONCHITO

        WHERE DOES FREEDOM LIVE ?
        WHY DO YOU DENY THE WIND ?

*   SILENT ONE

72

* AGIYA
BRINGER OF DREAMS
HOW SWEET YOUR VOICE TONES
FLOATING ACROSS TIME

HOW SACRED
PROFOUND LOVE IS
WHEN LEFT ALONE
TO THE WARM WINDS

* MY BELOVED /
CHEROKEE

SHE TURNS THE LIQUID IN MY BODY
INTO MOVING RIVERS
OF ENDLESS BOUNCING BUBBLES

MOONLIGHT RAIN

YOUR ENDLESS LIQUID
STAYS BLUE & FLOWING
& SWIRLS WITH PURPLE
MOMENTS /
& DIAMOND TEARS

HER LOVE CRASHES OVER ME
LIKE STORM HURRICANE WAVES
ON A ROCKY NEW ENGLAND COAST
IN A COLD DRIVING RAIN

YOUR SILENT MYSTERY
CONDENSES ME

LADY OF MY HEART
SEE ME
FREE ME

BLACK AS THE NIGHT
                              WOMYN
    BLACK AS THE NIGHT
    I TRAVEL
                    DREAM THE STARS
WITH YOU DREAM BODY
OF BLACKNESS

78

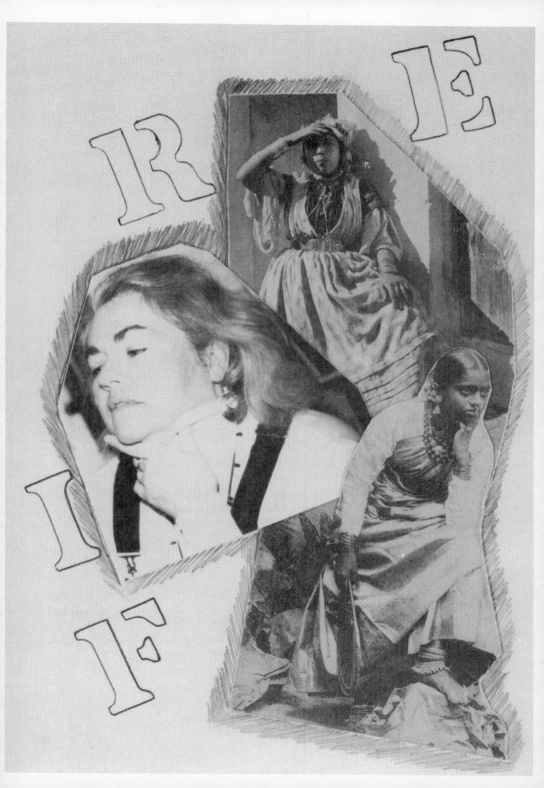

I LIVE AMONG EXQUISITE SHADOWS
SHE TRAVELS DISTANT PORTS

THE SPRING CAME UP FLAMES
MADDENING WARM WINDS
BREATHING OUR DISCONTENT   INTO
GARDENS OF ENDLESS
MOONLIGHT

& OUT OF THE WHIRLWIND
& THE TORONADO
SHE BLAZES ACROSS SKIES
OF OTHER COLORS
IN A DESERT
WHERE RAIN IS FALLING   /
BLACK SKY
& FINITE OPENING   /
PALM TREES BENDING
OVER TOUCHING THE EARTH   /

& THEN SHE'S GONE

                    /

I'M ALONE WITH
MY REGGAE MEMORIES

EMPTINESS IS STRENGTH

TO WALK ALONE INTO
OTHER DIMENSIONS

SWEETNESS FLEEING TO
THE DISTANT RECESSES
OF THE UNIVERSE
        CHALLENGING ME
        EXPANDING ME
        TO REACH
        FOR A WORLD
CUT OFF FROM ESOTERIC WALKERS

I'M TRAVELING IN THE BEYOND

I AM DIVING FOR THE ILLUSIVE
                    THREADS

I AM WEAVING THE COLORS OF
THE EARTHWALK
TO THE SILVER GREYS OF
BLUE PLANETS
IN DISTANT GALAXIES
& THE EMERALD CITIES ARE WAITING
FOR THE INHABITANTS

I AM POURING MY SOUL
INTO THE VOID OF THE DREAMERS

& WHEN I RETRIEVE IT
THE POWER OF FIVE CRYSTALS
CREATES THE LASER MOVEMENTS   /

YOU WALK IN FEAR

IF I REMOVE MY MASKS
YOU WILL BE IMAGED
IN THE MIRROR OF MY BEING

YOU WILL SEE YOUR OWN POWER

SOME TRIANGLES HAVE BEEN CARVED
INTO MY HEART

THEY HAVE GOLD & SILVER BORDERS

I REMAIN IN SILENCE
AT A POINT WHERE YOU STOPPED
TIME

YOU ARE METAPHOR FOR THE UNKNOWN
                    MYSTERIES
     FELT
          INTUITED
WHEN THE MIND LOSES
          THE STAIRWAYS
IN THE BRILLIANT   VIOLET/JADE
                    LIGHT

          YOU CARRY MESSAGES
               IN YOU TISSUES
     FROM OTHER WORLDS
     IN UNKNOWN LANGUAGES

86

BLUE GREY RIDGES
UNDERCUT
OCEAN WAVES
BEFORE
   THEY CRUSH YOU
ON THE WINDS OF TOMORROW
        /

I GAVE YOU MY SONG
IT WAS SACRED
YOU LEFT

I HONOR YOUR WARRIOR CHOICES
AS I HONOR MY WARRIOR PATH

YOU NO LONGER EXIST   /   FOR ME
YOU ARE GHOST

& MY MEMORY SLEEPS
IN A SILENT WIND
                              /

(ANDRÉ   /   WINTER . 9990)

88

I HAVE GONE   INTO TOMORROW
& TOMORROW HAS NEVER COME   /

& THE MOUNTAINS HAVE CALLED
DOWN THE THUNDER

WAS HER EXISTENCE
ONLY A THOUGHT
ON LONELY NIGHTS

WE MOVE ENERGY
TO ACHIEVE FREEDOM

PLEASURE IS AN ILLUSION
OF THE MOMENT
/

WHERE ARE THE ENTRANCES
WHERE ARE THE DEFINITIONS

I HAVE WALKED BEYOND ALL

THE CENTER MOVES   IMPERCEPTIBLY

SHE IS SEEKING
THE BORDERS
OF SPACE & INFINITY

HER LOVE FLOWS
SWEET & PURE
UNDISGUISED
BY THE LIMITS
OF TIME

WHEN YOU SEE THE LIGHTENING
                    FLASH
YOU WILL KNOW SHE IS THERE
WITH YOU
IN THE DESERT
OF YOUR
MIND

BRING THE DRUMS & RATTLES
FIRE WALKER
PURIFY MY SOUL
BEYOND THIS EARTHWALK

Bigwood Press
100 Grove Street
Worcester, MA 01605